I. D. K. CLUB BOOKLETS

General Editor
AUSTIN H. JOHNSON

No. I

THE SUPERSTITIONS OF
THE SCEPTIC

G. K. CHESTERTON

LONDON AGENTS:
SIMPKIN, MARSHALL, HAMILTON,
KENT AND CO., LTD.

THE SUPERSTITIONS

of the

SCEPTIC

GILBERT K. CHESTERTON

*With a Correspondence between the
Author and* MR. G. G. COULTON

CAMBRIDGE
W. HEFFER & SONS LTD.
1925

PRINTED IN GREAT BRITAIN

PREFACE

It is proposed from time to time to publish Addresses given to the I.D.K. Club, and also Essays, when it is felt they have some permanent or general interest. The Club is not committed to any sect or political party; it offers, in fact, a free arena for every sort of opinion, being concerned with the study of everything which may interest or benefit mankind.

Mr. Chesterton has kindly allowed us to open this series with his lecture, "The Superstitions of the Sceptic"; and this volume is printed from a shorthand verbatim report, together with a correspondence between the author and Mr. Coulton, the latter part by kind permission of *The Cambridge Review*, in whose columns the correspondence appeared.

The remarks which were concerned merely with the particular occasion and place of the delivery of the lecture have been omitted.

AUSTIN H. JOHNSON.

Cambridge,
  February, 1925.

THE SUPERSTITIONS OF THE SCEPTIC

I PROPOSE to start my rambling discourse by taking whatever has lately been said by Mr. Bernard Shaw and say the opposite. You will forgive me therefore if in this very disconnected discourse the starting point, and in a sense the text, is found in the recent work of my old friend and enemy. I suppose everybody here has heard of, and most people have probably either read or seen, the very interesting play called St. Joan; and I am not going to take up the function of the hundreds of young dramatic critics that I see before me by attempting to deal with it as a play, because my concern with it is only in one particular; but I will say by way of indicating my own general view of the subject that when I had read and seen it I wrote to my friend Bernard Shaw to ask him when his play on the subject of Joanna Southcott was coming out. That is a taunt which may appear to you somewhat cryptic and obscure, but it is really I think very relevant. You know that all sorts of things have been said about St. Joan of Arc at various periods. Shakespeare unfortunately represented her as a repulsive female adventurer; Voltaire, as something indescribable; Lord Byron said she was a fanatical strumpet; and Bernard Shaw has said that she was a Protestant progressive, and the founder as it were of the modern world. You will notice that it is only that last insult which is represented as having made her turn in her grave and rise indignant from the dead. None of the other descriptions of St. Joan, as far as I know, ever concerned themselves with the ghost of St. Joan returning to the earth—it required a further and terrible accusation to stir those sacred bones even in imagination; and the suggestion that she was responsible for the modern world was too much for anybody. But there is one particular passage in that play which will serve very well as a starting point for the little that I want to suggest this evening, and that is the fine passage of that very fair argument on the subject of persecution, in which the inquisitor, if I remember right, says, very truly as I think, that errors grow with an astonishing rapidity and with a bizarre variety that nobody could expect, and that some movement that began with an apparently well-meaning and simple man suggesting certain apparently more or less harmless things, will rapidly end with people committing some crime like infanticide, or insisting on going about without clothes. Now the only reason I am not going to discuss all the very interesting questions that are raised on that point in the argument is that it seems to me—and that is the point of my reference to Joanna Southcott—it seems to me that Bernard Shaw proves too much, I mean he proves too much for his own purpose, because he succeeds, I think, in convincing a fair and reasonable reader that if it was true that Joan of Arc stood for individualism in religion, and the right of each person to oppose his voice or his voices to the general sense of Christendom, if Joan of Arc meant that then she was wrong, and that is all.

I do not mean that I think she was wrong, but that Bernard Shaw thinks that she was wrong. There is nowhere in the whole of the play anything of the nature of a real answer to the Inquisitor or the Archbishop upon the common sense of the question. Joan of Arc does not prove that it would be a good thing for everybody to follow a purely individualistic religion; she does not attempt to. The argument really remains on the other side. In other words, if she did maintain that view, she was wrong, and if she maintained the view that anyone who has a psychical experience must trust that against common sense and against civilisation, to say nothing of any other authority—if she maintained that, she was wrong, wrong by the consensus of common sense people everywhere. Because as we all know there are a large number of people by this time hearing voices which sometimes say very singular things, and a great many of those people do so far illustrate the general subject that I am attempting to suggest this evening, that they were a great many of them at one time sceptics of the most complete sort. It is not specially of them that I want to speak this evening, but it is well to note as we pass that in the ordinary literal sense of the words we have seen a great many very great sceptics pass into what a good many of us at any rate would call very great superstitions. We have seen great men of science, for instance, who were agnostics or materialists, telling us things for which certainly the rationalists of the nineteenth century and still more of the eighteenth century could have found no term except raving madness. I mean men who doubted a great deal more than I ever doubted have come to believe more than I could possibly believe. We have seen people who thought it fantastical to believe that there could be a resurrection of a glorified body come to tell us of the resurrection of glorified niblicks and brassies for the purpose of playing a game of glorified golf. We have seen people who could not believe in the Sacramental mystery that was symbolised by the old legend of the Holy Grail, gravely tell us that people in the world of happy souls still have whiskies and sodas. It seems to me, by the way, rather characteristic of the rather third-rate character of that sort of religion, that they do say whiskies and sodas when they might at least be poetical and traditional and say ale or wine. But that is an unimportant point. I say merely in passing that we know the theory that each person should trust his psychical experience as an absolute, and ask for no other view and allow nothing to balance it or to moderate it at all; that view has developed very fully in the modern world, and most of us when we see it do not like it. It developed of course in a great many ways; apart from the present development of things like spiritualism it developed in a great many sects and leaders of various sorts; and that was what I meant when I asked Bernard Shaw why he shows this coldness, this neglect amounting almost to indifference, of the greatness of Joanna Southcott. Joanna Southcott is surely a far better example of pure individualism of religion, of a person who listens solely to her own voices, of a person who would not let any priest or council come between her and God; and she is, moreover, a person much nearer to us, our fellow country-woman, and we are not obliged in honouring her to do what

I know is always very painful to the friends of the international friendship of nations—pay a compliment to France. We are not obliged to go back a great many more years in the past than the life of Methusaleh in the future, and we have not reached things so remote or so obscure or so alien. We can find quite within our own time a great prophetess who stood up and declared with absolute clarity certain oracles of spiritual sources, and who has actually left her testament behind her; I believe there are some boxes or something that nobody has opened yet and they may contain news of prodigious spiritual value to the world. Why, in other words, if Bernard Shaw's ideal is the modern ideal, why does he have to go back to the medieval world to get it? And why does he describe in the play of Methusaleh infinite ages stretching forward into conditions that seem to me to be full of more and more depression, and have to go back 500 years to find inspiration and hope? The reason, I take it, is that all common sense people are really now agreed that the mere individual mysticism that relies upon the internal voices and nothing else is certainly wrong ninety-nine times that it is right once, and is when left to itself an anarchical and insane element in society. But I do not speak specially of those cases like that of Joanna Southcott, except in passing, because the thing I have to deal with this evening is not the ordinary excesses or extravagances of belief, but a certain element of credulity that strangely enough seems to me to come with and to a large extent to arise out of the mode of scepticism. As I say, it is illustrated sufficiently well in actual fact in the case of the remarkable appearance of scientists as spiritualists. But I am not dealing with that, but with something that is considerably more difficult to describe; and I must ask your indulgence if I do not make it as clear as I should wish to, because it is a rather large question and one that covers several centuries, and requires something like a little historical imagination, I think, to see it as a whole. When St. Joan was dead and the medieval order broke up, we all know that for good or evil there did come into the world an intellectual and religious disruption, whether we call it variety or anarchy, or by the language of praise or blame—call it if you like individualism; and to a very great extent it was not only individualism, but scepticism. Now when the Inquisitor in Bernard Shaw's play, whose words I have taken as a text, says that if you allow people spiritual individualism, without *sang froid* as it were, and without anything to balance it, you will have wild things like people walking about without clothes; he said something that has been illustrated often enough in human history. It seems to me in a certain sense he rather understates the case, because the thing that I wish to point out to you this evening is that when you leave everything in a more or less sceptical and undecided condition, what happens is not necessarily, or perhaps even generally, extravagance and madness, but in a sense the very opposite. What happens is constraint and servitude, that is to say, that one of the immediate results of cutting loose is, for some reason that I do not understand, that you chain yourself up again and chain yourself much more completely. In other words, whatever the old system of Christendom may have been and whatever we think of it, it is historically true that when people broke away from it they showed a most mysterious disposition for rushing, apparently of their own free will, into prisons and lunatic asylums, especially lunatic asylums, but lunatic asylums are prisons; and it is that aspect of them I am thinking of especially at the moment. It is as if one were to write a story about a man who had the rather nervous job of leading along on some journey a companion who had a morbid mono-mania for going to prison. One could imagine rather an amusing story made out of it, how you had to get him past police stations as they get drunkards past public houses. Something of that mysterious impulse seems for some reason or other to exist in the human intellect when it is emancipated or made sceptical or detached, or whatever phrase you may use; and I want very rapidly, if it does not bore you, to point out how curiously that has happened again and again in the last two or three centuries of our era.

Of course the first and most obvious example is that when the intellect was as it were left floating loose— and it must always be remembered that I have no intention of going into it in any detail—it must always be remembered as a historical fact that the interregnum of the Renaissance and of the general system of the sixteenth and seventeenth centuries was very much of an intellectual interregnum. That is to say, there was a considerable period before the formation of a possible new system like the Puritan system, a period during which large numbers of people were floating about very much as they are floating about in the world to-day, people whose spirit I suppose was represented by

Montaigne or by some of the Italian cultured sceptics of the time; and therefore you did have a period when there was a great deal of what one may call scepticism in the air, and the final form of modern Europe had by no means been yet taken.   What happened for instance in the countries like our own and in Scotland and in parts of Germany and in Holland, was a very extraordinary thing, which Matthew Arnold, you remember, summed up by saying the English people entered the prison of Puritanism and had the key turned on them for 200 years.   It is perhaps an exaggeration to say the English people entered it, and it is perhaps an exaggeration to say they were there for 200 years. But it may be stated, broadly speaking, as true.   You will notice that Matthew Arnold, who was certainly detached and in many ways in sympathy with the change, used also the word "prison," which is the key of what I am insisting on.   A large mass of people became so extraordinarily interested, for some reason that I have never quite understood, in one particular thin thread of argument, the logical argument from the omnipotence of God to the full Calvinist doctrine of predestination—became so extraordinarily interested in that one particular piece of Calvinistic logic, that they did to a very great extent transform the whole of social life as far as they could with a new atmosphere and a new spirit, and put upon themselves all kinds of very real and very rigid limitations.   I will not go into all those, because it raises rather an old controversy which is not really relevant; but it is enough to say that it is quite obvious that the people did feel the bonds as bonds.   I am not sneering at them for that.

Every man who has a religion feels some of its bonds as bonds at certain moments. But I am pointing out that these people had drifted into a system of which the bondage was very severe indeed. Nobody can read any of the great Puritans like Milton, etc., without feeling that there is a distinct resistance or struggle of Puritan humanity against the limits of the new system. But all I am concerned to point out in connection with this argument is that what had landed them in that severe and gloomy system overshadowed a vast part of our people until a very short time ago. If you read almost all of the great nineteenth century humanitarians, people like Dickens or Hood, or any of the hundred others who lived to preach a more generous and liberal conception of human pleasure, you will almost always find that they talk of the last generation as having been practically Calvinistic. They talk of the life of the old home or the family traditions, as if they were Puritanical in the most gloomy degree. Therefore I say that that influence—a very restricting influence—was (and that is the point which I am concerned with here) the direct immediate result of breaking loose, and what was called thinking for yourself. It was their religious liberty that created their social slavery.

Now the time came towards the end of the seventeenth century when it became increasingly obvious that this gloomy and grinding creed was not going to be permanently borne, and people began to break away from it in various ways, to break out of the prison into which they had entered voluntarily, to break with great difficulty out of the prison they had built for themselves; and you get at the end of the seventeenth century and the beginning of the eighteenth the full growth of modern scepticism in the ordinary sense of the word, the spirit that applies—as it is conceived—the humane and rational test to everything, and refuses superstitions and arbitrary doctrines and all the rest of it. Now I am going studiously to refrain in this discussion as far as I can from any terms that can be called terms of abuse as distinct from terms of history. I could say a vast deal about the Puritans, and the sort of things that a great many people said about the Puritans when they were there, the kind of things that Ben Jonson said; but I am not abusing any of these people; I am trying to trace the course of what always seemed to me a rather curious course of events. In the same way as I am not attacking the Puritans, so I am not attacking the Deists or the Sceptics of the eighteenth century. On the contrary, it always seems to me that there was something rather beautiful and touching about that brief interlude of contented Paganism, during which men thought for a very short time indeed that they could be wholly satisfied with this earth and this life. Bitter as Voltaire was, and foul as he often was, there is about some of his utterances also the suggestion of a curious innocence. When he said, "After all, a man must cultivate his garden," it always gives me a certain feeling as if it was the garden of Eden—that curious interlude when man believed that this earth was Eden, and that by being ordinarily humane and reasonably logical and practical, all problems would solve themselves. As I say, there is something beautiful about it, beautiful because it is dead and dead for ever. I heard a story the other day about a little boy who was asked to give an account of the story of the Garden of Eden, and said, "Adam and Eve lived in a beautiful garden, and they were perfectly happy until the servant came." That seems to me to be one of the few stories of children's blunders that sounds as if it was really made by a child, and it happens in this case to be something of a parable, because one of the many reasons that that optimistic interlude, which might truly be called the age of reason, one of the reasons why that optimistic interlude was after all an illusion, and therefore a fleeting thing, was that it was really in its social and economic aspect an aristocratic thing. The great Republican Deists of the eighteenth century— many of them in my opinion very fine men indeed—were most of them, among other misfortunes, gentlemen, and they were gentlemen of the sort who lived in a considerable degree of ignorance of the condition of the rest of the world. And you will generally find that their philosophy implies a great deal of leisure and not infrequently a great deal of learning. In short, that interlude which may be called the age of reason is in its best and most dignified aspect something like a kind of romance of youth, a romance of happiness; one may say I think that the only thing to be said against the age of reason is that it comes before the age of discretion. And that brief interlude of happy scepticism was followed by something else that arises out of its aristocratic character, and its quality of leisure and of learning and not infrequently of pedantry, and that was of course the gradual emergence of the tremendous popular problems of to-day. The problems appeared even to the men of the French Revolution as very much more

simple than they are—they appeared to them as we all
know rather as political than as economic, and though
they stood in many cases for very great truths, the
broader truth I think is that it was impossible to
maintain, to go on maintaining, that detached and
dignified attitude of the philosophical gentlemen of the
early and middle eighteenth century. What followed
was something else again. The mind was apparently
quite detached and emancipated again. It was perfectly
open to it to do anything or to do nothing, and what it
did once more was to build a prison; it set to work to
create out of that very rationalism that had been its
sort of holiday and romance—to build up that extraordinary structure, the full individualistic commercial
theory. It has many names; it was called at its earliest
stage Utilitarianism; it afterwards came to be called
the Manchester School. But the peculiarity of it that
I wish to point out was that it was very, very hard in
its dogmas indeed, that it limited men on all sides,
that it repressed all kinds of impulses that they would
naturally have, such as the impulse of pity, not to
mention the impulse of social indignation; and all
objections to it were answered exactly as Calvinists
would have answered objections to their creed, with the
repetition of an iron dogma. Everyone knows the
way in which good and honest men like Cobden and
Bright found it impossible upon their principles to do
so simple a thing as to forbid little children to be tortured
in factories. They said—and again I am not despising
the rigidity of the man who professes these dogmas—
he is in many ways an object of respect—they said, "We
have this fixed principle; the State must not interfere

in these things," and they therefore refused an action which I think would have been consonant to them and all other decent people as far as their instincts were concerned. In other words, you have again the same paradox, as it were, appearing; that which was constraining them, which was preventing them from doing ordinary things such as saving a child from torment or giving a penny to a beggar in the street—what was preventing them from doing this was not an ancient tradition or creed, but the cast-iron new system which they had made themselves, the last discovery of economic science. It was their free thought that forbade them free action. Therefore twice you have exactly the same thing repeating itself—a people supposed to be free and independent in the intellect, elaborately constructing a system that constrained themselves and constrained them far more inhumanly and harshly than had any older system in the remote past—something that restrained ordinary impulsive natural virtues. It was not religion that constrained Cobden and Bright; it was not even their Bibles and their Bible type of religion; on the contrary, their Bibles must have been a considerable embarrassment to them in that particular problem, because by a curious coincidence one of those very doctrines that they had inherited from the last prison, the last cast-iron system, the Puritan system, one of the very things they had inherited from that, the doctrine of the Sabbath, was itself an illustration of the thing of which they disapproved. It was a limitation of hours of labour. So that leaving on one side such trifles as the idea of being just to the poor or loving your neighbour, or unimportant things of that sort, even the sacred principle of the Sabbath really contradicted the theory of the Manchester School. But they remained true to that theory, and a great many other people did too. Now since that time we have seen possibly a still more extraordinary thing. First of all you have the gloomy unworldly religion of Puritanism established by people as a prison for themselves. Those people escaping from that, proceeding to build another prison, staying for a little while in rationalistic optimism, and then building for themselves another prison of which the whole system was that this world and material money considerations were the key to everything, and above all that that prosperity was to be obtained by ruthless competition and by an absolute refusal of anything like social authority. I may remark, because it is often forgotten, that the full doctrine of the Utilitarians was something much more extraordinary than many people now imagine, much more extraordinary than any tradition of old-fashioned radicalism to-day, because very great men indeed, like Adam Smith, laid down in effect the doctrine that if everybody followed his own self-interest the net result would be some degree of social happiness; that is to say, they preached a curious kind of cynical optimism whereby if everybody was for himself, God and not the Devil would in some way look after all the rest. That theory was preached as a philosophy and a hard and fast philosophy, and had all the stringency of a religion as we see when we find people refusing to do ordinary benevolent actions because they are against that religion.

Since then we have seen a still more extraordinary thing. We have seen the whole of that process reversed entirely; the Manchester School theory, the theory of Utilitarianism, or whatever you call it, broke down somewhere about the time when I was a child, and in the world in which I grew up people had already got used to saying that that was all nonsense, and they were therefore for the moment for a third time in that intermediary position of intellectual independence. They were no longer frightened of factory acts and charity, and they were to a certain extent free to maintain what they liked. What they did was to react to the opposite extreme and immediately to erect that into a new system which was made of iron and could not be altered, and which was full of dogmas. We call it the system of Karl Marx; broadly speaking, just as I am not abusing the Puritans or the Deists or the Utilitarians so I am not going to abuse the Bolshevists, but just to describe them and to say that everybody who has ever met a real Bolshevist or Socialist of the real Marxian tradition will agree with me in saying that he has again that same characteristic of an iron rigidity and a refusal to do anything whatever, however apparently humane, generous or natural or instinctive, which conflicts with the few fixed dogmas of his economic system. Therefore as I say, you have had three or four times (many more times, no doubt, if you went into detail)—at least three times we have had that curious experience of people who, by all, in the religious sense were supposed to be perfectly free and independent, laying upon themselves superstititions and slaveries, tying themselves up in knots that nobody had put upon them, like a man who whenever he was let out of the front door immediately tied himself to a tree or chained himself to the railings.

Only at very slight moments, passing moments, has there been anything resembling a really independent scepticism. The sceptics themselves have always turned something else into a sacred object, into a superstition, and when that thing was examined it was always found to be far narrower than the older traditions that had been rejected.

In conclusion, I should like to say that there is yet another development in that curious state of things. When people emerge in this fashion in the modern world, after all this succession of building their own prisons and destroying their own prisons, and then building more prisons—when they emerge from that they emerge in a curiously chaotic state of mind in many ways, and nothing is more notable about it than the fact that they continue to hold a large number of doctrines some of them quite true, but to hold them as superstitions, that is to say, in the strict sense, to hold them without reason. I alluded at the beginning of my remarks to that phrase of Bernard Shaw's of people going about without clothes. You will see a good deal of discussion in the newspapers nowadays about people who are going about with very few clothes, and nothing I think is more remarkable in that discussion than to notice the fact that nobody has the slightest idea of what he really holds on the subject. The whole argument is a chaos of sentimentalism. Some people say, if it is natural it is beautiful; other people say if it is beautiful it is right if it is ugly it is wrong, and the argument as used would lead, in the hands of any logician, in ten minutes to the obvious conclusion that nobody ought to wear any clothes at all. We all know that the vast mass of us would never go in for, let us say, individual moral emancipation to that extent or in that form; something constrains us, and I think it would be fair to say that it is a tradition—in ninety-nine people out of a hundred it is a tradition; in the strictly intellectual sense it is a superstition. It is a superstition because the modern world does not know why it keeps up these old same traditions of society. I know, for instance, why *I* believe in wearing clothes; I believe in it because I believe in the fall of man, which does not mean merely the story of Adam and Eve, but the highly practical and profound philosophy which teaches us that in man what is natural is not necessarily beautiful, and certainly not necessarily good; that there are all sorts of elements and potentialities in man that can no more be trusted than Bengal tigers or storms at sea. I am only pointing out to you that I who hold certain doctrines have reasons for my conventions and decencies (so far as I observe conventions and decencies)—but such as I have, I have reason for. Now the vast mass of the sceptical modern world has no reason at all for its conventions. Suppose I suddenly say, "What is the matter with cannibalism?" most of you will simply say that it isn't nice—and you will be quite right. I am not sneering at tradition, I am not sneering at it even when I call it superstition; but I say that to the vast majority of people in a modern civilised state, cannibalism is in more senses than one a matter of taste. It is at bottom the fact that you do not fancy a slice of missionary. Now there again the whole human race, because of its sanity, its instincts, its traditions, which embody that sanity in these things, does in fact know in practice that it is not going to be cannibal; but in a strictly intellectual sense the attitude is superstitious, because in nine cases out of ten it does not know why it disapproves of cannibalism. I know why I disapprove of it—I disapprove because I believe that man is the image of God, and that he is different from the brutes in a fundamental and real sense and that his dignity must be preserved by a separation. But how many thousands of people nowadays have mixed up men and animals past any separation or any distinction. How many of them have anything like a religious dogma or even a clear ethical dogma distinguishing man from the other creatures. Yet all of them have the instinct that a man is different from a brute, and therefore that they do not propose to eat their grandmother in the economical manner of the Sandwich Islands. But the thing upon which that idea rests is, believe me, in almost all of you a tradition; I do not say of *you*, because no doubt this room is filled exclusively with clear-headed logicians who have thought out all their first principles; but shall we say people in the street outside—many of them do not know why they believe in wearing clothes, and do not know why they do not believe in eating men. And the reason is that they inherited from these old dogmatic systems that they have thrown away, various fragments, most of them true but inherited from the old systems they have cast aside; they no longer know what their own foundations are, and if they trace back all those noble and honourable prejudices to their really logical origin, I think in nine times out of ten they will find that they were rooted in the Christian Faith.

THE CORRESPONDENCE

between

The Author and Mr. G. G. Coulton

THE CORRESPONDENCE

between

The Author and Mr. G. G. Coulton

MR. CHESTERTON'S HISTORY

Mr. G. G. Coulton

Mr. Chesterton lectured to us on Monday night upon "The Superstitions of the Sceptic." When requested to give medieval evidence for what he implied about the Middle Ages, he replied that it was the questioner's business to produce that evidence, and promised that he would meet this as publicly as it might be produced. I will therefore print as much as the Editor's space allows. I need not here give references; having done so in other volumes *ad libitum* or (as unfriendly critics might say) *ad nauseam*; I may fairly throw upon Mr. Chesterton the onus of contradicting my assertions and calling for further proof, at the risk of further exposing himself by such contradictions.

He told us, with regard to the Reformation: "One result of cutting loose is that you chain yourself more completely. The reformers entered into prisons of their own. . . . The English people entered the prison of Puritanism. . . . I could say a vast deal about the Puritans [but I don't want to spend my time abusing them]. I am trying here to trace a rather curious course of events. . . . It puzzles me to trace this course of events [in the history of Puritanism]."

I took down these words, I think I may safely claim, *verbatim*, except those in brackets, which I had only time to paraphrase.

Questions were invited, and these references to Puritanism, chosen from among others which invited almost equally direct historical criticism, formed the subject of discussion. Mr. Chesterton was asked whether he could specify a single point in seventeenth century Puritanism (apart from the doctrine of Predestination, upon which Puritans themselves often differed) which was not also orthodox in the Middle Ages. The reply, which was not easy to follow, implied that monks and ascetics were the only orthodox medieval Puritans; that general Church teaching was free then from all Puritanical taint; and especially that the Middle Ages were ages of dance and innocent mirth. It is with that presentment that we are concerned here. Let us take the typical prescriptions of orthodox medieval Churchmen *for the laity*, quite apart from the monastic ideal. And let us take first the subject on which Mr. Chesterton was so emphatic, and on which, as he said in almost as many words, he was telling his hearers only things which were familiar to everybody who had studied actual medieval records. Let us take the medieval dance.

I know of only two or three exceptional Churchmen in the Middle Ages who make even the most grudging allowance for dancing as compatible with Christian morals. Quite typical is that sentence from Augustine which is repeated from Churchman to Churchman down the Middle Ages, that it is less sinful even to plough on

Sundays than to dance. The friars themselves, though they of all the clergy (except those humble parish parsons whose voice has scarcely ever come down to us) had most sympathy with the village folk—even the friars are dead against dancing. Dancers are anti-christian, a Church of Malignants; they are possessed with devils; they dance to the ruin of their souls. They are worse than the Jews; for these shrank from crucifying Christ on a feast-day, yet it is precisely the feast days of the Church which men choose for dancing. One remedy against dancing is "the remedy of fear and reason; to wit, that we should reflect how this place wherein we are set is a valley of tears and not of dancing, of wretchedness and not of song." Dancers should be forcibly restrained by their parents and masters; they should be deprived of the finery in which they dance, "as we singe a cat's skin lest she should go caterwauling abroad." They should even be beaten if recalcitrant; it was Eli's ruin that he did not beat his unruly sons. The clergy have a right to keep them from the dance, "even as the King's ministers might restrain their subjects from conspiring against the King."

Mr. Chesterton has evidently never realised how strongly St. Francis's love of song and mirth at certain moments contrasts, not only with the religious world of his day, but even with the ordinary and reflective St. Francis, the St. Francis who did not run naked about the streets—for by another strange slip, he implied to us that running naked was a product of post-reformation religious imagination, and forgot one of the most striking episodes in the career of a saint whose biography Mr. Chesterton himself has put upon the modern market.

Again, one of the most Franciscan of the early friars
(outside the circle of contemporaries who had known the
saint personally), is Berthold of Regensburg, whom
Roger Bacon commends as the greatest popular preacher
of the thirteenth century. Berthold quotes Augustine's
words against the dancers, and only adds as a qualifi-
cation that folk may dance "at bridals" without sin.
Otherwise, they risk mortal sin; he who dies in mortal
sin goes inevitably to hell; a sudden heart-failure in our
partner's arms would land us forthwith in a place in
which we shall be a thousand times more uncomfortable
than if the whole universe were at white-heat, and we
white-hot in the midst of it; these tortures will be
increased a thousandfold again at the Last Day, when
every man will come to his final reward; then they will
last for as many years as all the hairs that have ever
grown on all the beasts that have crawled on this earth
since God first made Adam—and even then, we shall be
only at the beginning of our pains. Moreover, as
Aquinas and all the great schoolmen agree, the blessed
in heaven will take pleasure in the contemplation of these
our agonies; not as uncharitable towards us, but
accidentaliter, as a glorious object-lesson of the Justice
of God.

It was not quite so sinful merely to take pleasure in
other folks' dancing. The sister of one of the greatest
Roman saints suffered only fifteen days of purgatory
"because once, standing in mine own chamber, I listened
with a certain sweetness to the songs of them that danced
in the streets, for which I did no penance during my
earthly life; wherefore I must now be punished for
fifteen days in purgatory." But then Albert the Great,

Aquinas's master, is reported to have said from experience that he would rather have been roasted alive with St. Laurence than bear one moment more of the purgatorial flames.

This attitude towards the dance far outlasted the Reformation in Roman Catholic countries; a devout parish priest thought to earn praise from Fénelon for having put down the dance in his parish; in the villages subject to the great abbey of St. Peter in the Black Forest, the customal prescribes: "The parson has the right of forbidding dancing; and when he chooses to prohibit all dance, then every dancer pays a fine of three shillings, be it man or woman."

In the face of this, and masses of similar evidence, must we not conclude that the course of events which so puzzles Mr. Chesterton is fairly simple? The seventeenth century puritans tried to enforce what the medieval Church had preached, but failed to enforce, often even winking at infractions. Their psychology may have been very defective, but *on these points of theology* they were orthodox medievalists; they agreed with St. Bernard and with at least nine-tenths of St. Francis.

Let us therefore now put to Mr. Chesterton a counter-question framed on his own lecture. Can he name a single man of science, who, having gained a great reputation and a rich income by science, is superstitious enough to believe that he could write (for instance) a History of England out of the merest journalistic scraps of historical information? Have not such ventures of faith been mainly characteristic of brilliant littérateurs? Goldsmith's histories became a byword almost in the author's lifetime; and they would lie still deeper in the literary hell if Goldsmith had written them to serve a religious sect.

Mr. Chesterton will doubtless remember the story (I quote from memory) of Henry Fielding, who once staved off a few bills more hastily than usual by writing another play after methods even more offhand than his wont. The manager, after the first rehearsal, found the author tobacconing (as our ancestors called it) by the tavern fire, and protested with great concern: "This will never do, Mr. Fielding." The author blew a ring, and replied philosophically: "Well, let the fools find it out!" Then came the first night, and a storm of hisses, and a desperate, incoherent manager bursting in again upon the author, still tobacconising by the same tavern fire. Then Fielding, who had something not only of Mr. Chesterton's literary genius, but also of his imperturbable bonhomie, blew another ring, and remarked: "So the fools *have* found it out, have they?" We still read *Tom Jones*; but that play is probably read, if at all, only as a curiosity in literary history.

G. G. COULTON.

Nov. 11, 1924.

[From *The Cambridge Review*, November 14, 1924.]

MR. G. K. CHESTERTON'S REPLY

SIR,—It is a very great honour for a journalist to find his views criticised at all by so distinguished a scholar as Mr. Coulton, and I should like to begin with two apologies to him; the first for the delay in this reply, which was due to my being forced to go wandering in Scotland when his criticism was sent to me, and the second for the circumstances of our too brief public conversation, to which he refers. I am very sorry, but not very much surprised, if he only imperfectly understood my answers; for the truth is that I rather imperfectly heard his questions, which was due perhaps to some acoustical accident, if I may make the guess without being a professor of acoustics.

Mr. Coulton, I fear, thinks me a very frivolous person, yet, in truth, I did not venture upon guesses and generalisations about history without considering somewhat seriously the problem that it raises, touching the inevitable inferiority of the amateur to the specialist. It seems to me a rather difficult problem, with difficulties for the specialist as well as the amateur. My critic has complimented me with a comparison to Goldsmith, and certainly there is more real English history in ten lines of *The Deserted Village* than in the whole of Hume. But it is the very depth and darkness of my ignorance that discloses the difficulty. I am willing to believe that not only Mr. Coulton, but every other man I meet in Cambridge knows much more than I do. But in that case how inconvenient and incalculable must be my course and progress through the Cambridge streets. I must become a modernist after meeting one man, a medievalist after meeting the next. The man in the street must be wholly at the mercy of an academic priesthood. When the priests quarrel, he cannot even cling to the most learned; for he cannot know which is the most learned without being more learned than all of them. And as there are specialists about everything, it is impossible for any ordinary person to form any impression about anything. Even a Protestant priesthood will hardly demand so complete a surrender of private judgment. I have reflected; and I think I see the place of the amateur.

The obscure things, the details and disputed points, the great scholar can always see and note better than we can. It is the obvious things that he cannot see. I do not say this in mere depreciation; I think it is really inseparable from that concentrated research to which the world owes so much. It is the truth in the traditional picture of the absent-minded professor, who remains gazing at a fossil or a Roman coin and fails to observe external objects, such as a house on fire, a revolution, an escaped elephant putting its head through the skylight, and similar things. Mr. Coulton's view of history shows the same limitations; and it is precisely because I am so much less learned than he that it is my privilege to lead him through common ways, pointing out elephants and other enormous objects. For instance, inferior as I may be in information about the medieval world, I have as much right as anyone else to form impressions of the modern world. And I can hardly trust myself blindly to one who really seems to believe (as does Mr. Coulton) that the field of "science" is free from journalistic adventures, amateur experiments, quacks and charlatans, even as this Chesterton. A man must indeed be imprisoned in the medieval world, if he does not know that the big public event in modern science has been the stepping of great specialists like Sir Oliver Lodge into fields where their foes can call them charlatans. Similarly, I can only regard with respectful amazement the spectacle of a capable and cultivated gentleman, walking about in broad daylight in modern Europe, and still quite honestly under the impression (I quote his very words) that the Catholic Church is a religious sect.

The first obvious question is what it is all about. If there is one medieval superstition which I admire more than another it is the habit of our barbarous ancestors of making it quite clear what they were trying to prove. I am not sure that I know what Mr. Coulton is trying to prove; and I am pretty sure he does not know what I am trying to prove. In the case at issue, my lecture at Cambridge, he knows so little what I am trying to prove that he actually helps me to prove it. The brilliant specialist is here so blind to the obvious that he does not even know what he himself is doing; in the sense of what he is demonstrating. The thesis of my lecture (if he will pardon the medieval pedantry of logic) was this: that the Reformation was followed, not by the intellect finding freedom, but by its building new and often narrower prisons. As the first of several examples, I mentioned Puritanism. My critic merely suggested, in his question, that there was nothing in Puritanism that there was not in Medievalism, with the exception of predestination. In his letter he merely suggests that the Puritans only applied medieval principles, apparently with more thoroughness. Here, again, he shows a curious innocence about what he is proving. All that this could possibly prove is that Catholics were capable of the Renaissance and Protestants were not; or in other words that the Puritans dragged the world back when the Popes let it go forward. As I am not a "medievalist" but a Catholic, I should not quarrel very much with him for making out this case. But anyhow he has made out my case. His letter substantially supports my lecture. By his own account, the Puritans restored austerity with the addition of predestination. So far from finding freedom, they forged more efficient chains with at least one additional chain; Q.E.D.

Now I have never failed to confess freely that I am ignorant of many such details as my critic adduces about dancing; though I am not ignorant of the way in which such details can be selected and arranged by the most honest partisan. But even by the details as he gives them, that some moralists allowed dancing, that some allowed it at weddings, that some disallowed it on Sundays, I can see that the case was not so simple as he suggests; I recognise that Catholic atmosphere of living complexity that came to be called casuistry. Probably it is what he means by mentioning (though not explaining) the Church's habit of "winking"; but he seems to admit that the puritan never indulged in anything so frivolous as a wink. But why did the Church wink? However he explains it, he can only bring out my conclusion; that the schismatics did not find freedom but more constraint.

And now for the general matter. In my verbal reply, which he says was not easy to follow, I merely recited what I should have thought he would have recognised as the ordinary Catholic theory of different vocations; but if he had, he would hardly have translated it as "monks and ascetics" being "the only orthodox medieval Puritans"; or said that it implied in itself that the Middle Ages were ages of dance and innocent mirth.

Indeed, he himself says that this was merely an implication. It seems to me odd that a man should base his whole complaint, not on what was said, but what he thinks was implied, in a sentence that he could not follow. But anyhow I did not say, and do not imply what he imagines; certainly not what he answers. I do not maintain that medieval priests went about like the new nonconformist preachers, teaching people the Joy of Life. It never needs to be taught except in depressed and debilitated communities. I do not maintain that medievalism was all beer and skittles, or mostly beer and skittles, though I note, as Cobbett did, that it sometimes condemned men to fast on beer and bread. For instance, I should never have expected a scholar to glance at anything so plain and popular as my little book on St. Francis. But I think it strange that any scholar so acute should look at anything so plain without understanding what it says. Mr. Coulton talks as if I ignored the asceticism of St. Francis and his age, and connected him merely with art and song. Having written a whole book almost entirely to show that St. Francis *was* an ascetic, and *not* (as his modern admirers suggest) merely a votary of art and song, I cannot but accept this result of my effort with a gentle sigh.

Anybody can look and see what I did say about a general ascetical atmosphere that preceded and surrounded St. Francis and doubtless lingered long after him. I compared it to a black cave and a howling wilderness, to a world without stars or flowers, to the fires of purgatory and the fasts that cast out devils; and various other things not commonly identified with dance and Provençal song and sunburnt mirth. I do not see

how I could have put it more strongly; and I can only
respectfully hope that Mr. Coulton reads medieval books
more carefully than modern books. The only difference is that I gave something like a reasonable reason
for human beings behaving in so strange a way; whereas
he can only fall back on the old unhistorical Protestant
method of treating it as a nightmare from nowhere.
And that brings me to the vital point at issue. The
general thesis I should maintain might be stated thus:
"Medieval religion, including medieval asceticism, was
totally different from Puritanism, was indeed contrary to
Puritanism, and was certainly much less gloomy than
Puritanism. It was different in meaning, different in
motive, different in atmosphere and different in effect.
The two things were so diverse that even when they were
the same they were different; as different as a Catholic
and an atheist vegetarian when they both refuse meat on
Friday."

What is the matter with my critic's general view is
that it is incredible. It is incredible by a thousand
converging things that make up common sense. I will
choose only one at random. It is inconsistent with the
stark outstanding fact of the figure that the Puritan cuts
in history. I mean the effect of the Puritan, as it is felt
in life and literature. Men like Shakespeare and Ben
Jonson had fathers or grandfathers who must have
remembered the old medieval routine as it remained
after the Wars of the Roses. Even if the Renaissance
had penetrated every byeway of the north (which seems
most unlikely) the interruption must have been very
recent and very brief. Tradition must still have been
full of the momentum of the long medieval memories.

Under these circumstances, if the Puritans had only been like medieval priests, they would have been noticed as being like medieval priests. The tone of the comments on them would have been "Oh Lord, here are the dismal old shavelings back again." It was totally different. The tone of the comments was "Who ever heard of such nonsense as these new religious people are talking?" So Shakespeare's characters, who accept a friar as something familiar and presumably friendly, will talk of Malvolio being a Puritan as if it were a sort of monster. It is to me simply incredible, as a mere matter of human nature, that people should speak thus of a new thing if all the old things had been exactly like it. I believe that Mr. Coulton has done me the honour to say that I regard history as a branch of fiction. It is one of the talents of the scholar to discover truths that he does not understand. I have read one book of history to his hundred; but I have one advantage over him. I can read a book of history as naturally as if it were a novel. I can remember that it consists of human beings as real as those in a novel. Now suppose somebody applied this principle, say, to *David Copperfield*; suppose somebody said that Peggoty, being an old-fashioned nurse, had probably treated David quite as harshly as the Murdstones or Mr. Creakle. We should simply know it was not so; because, if it had been so, the stepfather's régime would never have seemed to David a new and unnatural reign of terror. Nor would the Puritans have been even felt as Puritans, if they had been the same as priests. This is a very good example of what I mean by the invisible elephant; the colossal lump of common sense that seems to be too large for

specialists to see. But this is only one of a thousand
such things, all pointing to the same common sense
conclusion. Why did the Puritan reformers carefully
cut out of the old theology exactly those things that
lent themselves to a more lenient treatment of lighter
weaknesses? Our Lady was popularly conceived as
almost illogically indulgent insinuating a finger on the
scale in the weighing of souls, saving the drunken monk
from the punishment of his folly. They cut her out.
Purgatory was conceived as the place of expiation for
venial sins, with a background of hope. They cut it out.
Why, putting aside secular things, were the colours
even of religious things so much more cheerful for the
medieval than for the Puritan? Why was a Catholic
prayer-meeting a gayer spectacle than a Puritan
banquet? All these and numberless other questions
will besiege the mind; but I must not take too much of
your space. I will conclude with the fundamental fact
that is the answer to them all.

The most obvious of all the obvious things is the
world a man lives in. The universe is the supreme
example of a thing that is too obvious to be seen; and
Mr. Coulton forgets all about it. He said that medievalism and Puritanism were much the same "except for
predestination," as if (heaven help us) it were a sort
of parenthesis. No man who says that as a parenthesis
understands religious history at all. The man who
separated himself from Christendom, to concentrate on
his one conviction of predestination, lived in a separate
universe. In one sense, perhaps, he was not so much
troubled as the priest about sin, because not so much
troubled about free-will. But his tone, his terminology,

his taste in colour and the rest were more sombre, simply because his sense of sin was a sense of doom. For it is always the fundamental things that are superficial; and subconscious convictions appear in the idiom and the voice. The chasm between the cosmic convictions is far more real than all the very disputable and variable casuistry about things like dancing. Even with the little knowledge I have, I could have guessed for myself that the majority of medieval moralisings would have deplored various dances in various degrees; in what precise degree Mr. Coulton does not make clear, for he seems to be unconscious of the difference between a sin and an occasion of sin. But suppose that, not many priests, or most priests, but all priests had denounced it, suppose (absurd as it is) that the Church denounced dancing as it does stealing, suppose any extravagance along the lines he mentioned . . . and still you would not be within a thousand miles of the thing we mean when we call Calvinism gloomy. You would not be in the same world with it. A Catholic theologian would have a good deal to say about the dancer who died of heart-failure and went to hell; and the simplification savours somewhat of Hyde Park. But the point is that a Calvinist theologian would simplify it in another and annihilating sense. The priest would only be warding off a blow of the devil in what was (in the most exact sense) a free fight. He would be the very antithesis of the Puritan; whose whole point was that God had made the man and the sin and the dance and the death and everything else, with the deliberate purpose of making the man dance his way to the devil for the divine glory. The Puritan was more gloomy, simply because this view is more gloomy. To

D

put it shortly, the ascetic only said, "The Day of Judgment is at hand." The Calvinist really said, "The Day of Judgment is *over*; let the earth keep silence before the Lord." That is the Scottish Sabbath. That is what is meant by living in a different world.

May I conclude by saying that, among the obvious things, there are indeed some things that are obvious to us and which we cannot expect to be obvious to him. Every Catholic of course understands quite easily, and from the inside, all the things that Mr. Coulton cannot even on his own principles explain. Every Catholic knows quite well why the huge power of the old Church was in fact felt as less oppressive than the brief *coup d'état* of the Puritans; why from the very colours of art or outline of architecture a man could tell the difference a mile off; why Catholicism showed a humanistic indulgence long before Protestanism; and why a thousand denunciations do not make one damnation.

But, broadly speaking, I will say this. Nobody will ever get any notion of what the Catholic Church is all about, if he is content to quote separate definitions because they sound very definite, and then make his own deductions from what he imagines that they mean. All Catholicism is a balance, made of definitions that correct each other and to some seem to contradict each other. The heretic, such as the Calvinist, is not a man who has this or that thought, but a man who separates himself from others that he may think of nothing else. Thus, if we were to take all modern Catholic sermons about peace, we should probably find the vast majority merely pacific and even platitudinous; very few of them directly supporting war. But anybody who inferred that

Catholics were exactly like Quakers, would have dis-
tressing adventures when he got among the Italians or
the Irish. The Quaker was not a man who loved peace
but a man who loved peace more than unity. The
Puritan was not merely a man who had elements of
Puritanism; he was a man who rejected all other
elements in order to have his Puritanism pure. There
might really seem at times to be something Calvinist
about a Catholic. But there was nothing Catholic about
a Calvinist. Calamity awaits anybody who tries to infer
from one dictum, without the balancing dictum, what
Catholics are like, instead of looking to see what they
are like. We might well take the gay apologue of
Mr. Coulton; the little idyll of hell, heart-disease and the
dance of death. If a dancer dropped down dead
shrieking blasphemies under all the conditions defined
as sending a man to the devil, Mr. Coulton (an ardent
but ill-instructed convert) would suddenly find himself
forbidden to say that the man had gone there. I daresay
he would be a little bewildered; but I don't blame him.
But there are inconveniences in writing the most learned
book about five centuries of religion without knowing
what the religion was.

Yours, etc.,
G. K. CHESTERTON.

[From *The Cambridge Review*, December 3, 1924.]
FR. JOHN LOPES WRITES

SIR,—In his article on "Mr. Chesterton's History" in
your issue of November 14, Dr. Coulton quotes St.
Thomas Aquinas as a representative medieval authority

on the subject of Hell.   May I ask him if he will accept
St. Thomas as an equally trustworthy witness to the
teaching of the medieval Church on the subject of
Dancing?   If so, the following passage would seem to
justify the careful distinction made by Mr. G. K.
Chesterton in his answer to Dr. Coulton's question on the
subject at the Guildhall lecture.

Yours, etc.,

JOHN LOPES.

2, Round Church Street, Cambridge.

"Deinde quaeritur de ludis chorealibus, utrum sine
peccato exerceri possint, propter illud quod dicit : 'Et
plaudebant': arguit enim hoc tamquam peccatum.

"Ad quod dicendum, quod ludus secundum se non
est malus; aliter in ludis non esset virtus quae dicitur,
eutrapelia: sed secundum quod ordinatur diverso fine,
et vestitur diversis circumstantiis, potest esse actus
virtutis et vitii.   Quia enim impossibile est semper
agere in vita activa et contemplativa; ideo oportet
interdum gaudia curis interponere, ne animus nimia
severitate frangatur, et ut homo promptius vacet ad
opera virtutum.   Et si tali fine fiat de ludis cum aliis
circumstantiis, erit actus virtutis, et poterit esse
meritorius, si gratia informetur.   Istae autem circum-
stantiae videntur in ludo choreali observandae: ut non
sit persona indecens, sicut clericus, vel religiosus; ut
sit tempore laetitiæ, ut liberationis gratia, vel in nuptiis,
et hujusmodi: ut fiat cum honestis personis, et cum
honesto cantu; et quod gestus non sint nimis lascivi, et
si qua hujusmodi sunt.   Si autem fiant ad provocandum
lasciviam, et secundum alias circumstantias, constat
quod actus vitiosus erit."

Sancti Thomae Aquinatis In Isaiam prophetam expositio. Caput Tertium. Omnia Opera. Vol. 14. P. 445. Parmae, MDCCCLXIII.

[As this is our last number this term, we have passed the above to Mr. Coulton, and print his reply in the next column.—Ed. C.R.]

[From *The Cambridge Review*, December 3, 1924.]

Mr. G. G. Coulton Rejoins

Sir,—I did not quote Aquinas as "a representative medieval authority"; on the contrary, he is the most moderate of the great schoolmen, and represents *the minimum* of medieval Puritanism; e.g. he is far less emphatic than his contemporary, St. Bonaventura, as to the pleasure felt by the blessed in watching the writhing of sinners in hell beneath their feet. And I am glad to see that he shows equal moderation in the matter of the dance; this is distinctly the least unfavourable judgment I have yet seen. Yet, even so, what does Aquinas allow? To avoid sin, the dance must be done "at a time of rejoicing, as, for instance, for the sake of liberation, or at weddings and such like; it should be done with respectable persons and respectable song," and so on. This is simply abbreviated from Aquinas's own master, Albert the Great (*in lib. IV. Sent.* dist. 16). In Albert, it is essential to morality that dances should be "at due time of rejoicing, as at weddings or in time of victory, or of a man's personal liberation or that of his country, or the home-coming of a friend from some far-off land." Neither Aquinas nor Albert think of suggesting the ordinary Sunday or holy-day as a time for lawful dances, and, indeed, later Church law explicitly excluded such occasions: "They who dance on Church holidays commit mortal sin," writes Luther's adversary and Aquinas's fellow-Dominican, Guillaume Pépin (*Destruct Ninive*, Serm. 17); and again: "It is not permitted to any of the faithful to dance publicly on holy-days or Sundays" (Richard et Giraud, *Bib. Sacrée* s.v. *danse*). Again, with regard to the "respectable songs," Albert is quite explicit: "That the songs and music which excite [the dancers] on such occasions should not be of the unlawful kind, but songs of moral matters or concerning God." There is nothing in Aquinas or Albert, therefore, which a Puritan like Milton could not have echoed; even Joanna Southcott would have permitted dance, with songs about God, on the day when the Bishops opened her Box. Aquinas is, no doubt, in full accord with Father Lopes' own moderate views, but I contend that he gives no justification whatever for the paradoxes with which Mr. Chesterton entertained us.

G. G. COULTON.

Nov. 29, 1924.

[From *The Cambridge Review*, December 3, 1924.]

MR. G. G. COULTON CONTINUES

SIR,—I find nothing of importance in Mr. Chesterton's five columns which does not depend upon his putting into my mouth things which I neither said, nor should have been likely to say, unless I had plunged very thoughtlessly into this important subject.

The issue is very simple.   Mr. Chesterton insisted on
Puritanism as a post-Reformation product; "it was
their religious liberty that created the social slavery";
therefore our discussion turned on the attitude of the
Medieval Church towards the dance. Since Mr.
Chesterton here complains that "Mr. Coulton does not
make clear" those degrees of casuistry about dancing
which he assumes to be "very disputable and variable,"
and since it is an academic prejudice at Cambridge that
one of two disputants should stick to the point, therefore
I crave for space for further quotations, which may
possibly entertain some of your readers.

Medieval casuistry about the dance is astoundingly
free from variation.   Fr. Lopes has printed what, so far
as he or I know, is the least unfavourable pronounce-
ment to be found among the whole mass of medieval
moralists; yet this goes no farther than the puritan
Milton would have gone.   The question here is not
whether there were good moral reasons for the prohibition
of the village dance, but simply whether that prohibition
was invented in the Middle Ages or in the sixteenth
century; and Mr. Chesterton needed only to look into
The Catholic Encyclopedia to realise how rash his own
assumptions were.   This *Encyclopedia*, guaranteed by
full ecclesiastical licence and imprimatur, does not dare,
even at the present day, to go beyond what Aquinas
and Milton would have allowed. (Vol. IV., p. 619.)
"As to social dancing, now so much in vogue, whilst in
itself it is an indifferent act, moralists are inclined to
place it under the ban, on account of the various dangers
associated with it.   Undoubtedly old national dances,
in which the performers stand apart, hardly, if at all,

holding the partner's hand, fall under clerical censure
scarcely more than any other kind of social intercourse.
But, aside from the concomitants—place, late hours,
décolleté, escorting, etc.—common to all such entertain-
ments, round dances, although they may possibly be
carried on with decorum and modesty, are regarded by
moralists as fraught, by their very nature, with the
greatest danger to morals." Four other Catholic
theological dictionaries say very much the same; it is
only the three Protestant dictionaries that are really
tolerant of the dance. But the most interesting of all
is a little monograph which I picked up on a French
bookstall: *Some Words about Modern Dances*, by le
Vicomte de St.-Laurent, who claims the support of the
Bishop of Bayeux. (3rd ed. Paris, 1857.) He treats
it as "a matter of life and death for Christian morality"
(p. 8). "Read Monsignor Bouvier's *Theology*; it will
teach you that the waltz is a mortal sin in itself. . . .
In fact, when the man is a Christian and his partner also,
his hand only leans flat against her waist, the edge of it
resting on the flounces of her crinoline. I consider this
fashion very immoral, but it is the decentest and rarest
fashion" (22—4). The waltz is tolerated because it is
a rich man's sin. "Ye poor peasants, whose dances
(less dangerous than this) are so often anathematised
by your priests from the pulpit, what do you say when
you see this same priest entertained at the château,
where the biggest landowner in the parish lets his town
friends dance and polk?" (34). The poor are saying
"Bah! the priests let the rich do what they like, in
order to get money out of them to build their churches!"
(62). And he protests, in words which might have come

from a medieval moralist, against the sin of winking in practice at what the Church condemns in theory (57—8). For here is the point at which I am least able to follow Mr. Chesterton. He defends "the Church's habit of 'winking'" at those dances which she publicly forbade; here, he says, "I recognise that Catholic atmosphere of living complexity that came to be called casuistry." If these words are to be taken seriously, and not merely as an embarrassed debater's improvisation, then the greatest Catholics of the Middle Ages would have repudiated his plea even more unreservedly, perhaps, than I do. I could easily fill a whole number of *The Review* with ecclesiastical prohibitions; and it astonishes me even in Mr. Chesterton that he should have had no inkling of these things when he undertook to write social history. Moreover, he seems equally ignorant of what the schoolmen really taught concerning predestination. How can one argue seriously with a sectarian advocate who complacently ignores the greatest scholars of his own sect in those far-off days when it included, with comparatively few exceptions, the ablest and most learned minds in Western Europe? For he must permit me to follow *The Oxford English Dictionary*, and to bracket his creed with other sects. The fact that he himself prefers to employ that term only as a reproach to outsiders does not really help him; on the contrary, your sectarian *par excellence* is your exclusivist, who calls other creeds by names which (he thanks God) cannot apply to his own. However, Mr. Chesterton may prefer to name things, these remain what they are; and he may learn from Bossuet, the greatest Catholic controversialist of all time, that "the worst intellectual vice is the vice of thinking that things *are*, just because *we should like them to be.*"

He "hopes I read medieval books more carefully" than I have read his *St. Francis*. I never read, nor pretended to have read, that book. I simply pointed out that this Guildhall lecturer, who ignored one of the most startling and familiar events in Francis's career, was one who had written a life of St Francis. Finally, he protests against non-Catholics even pretending to understand Catholics. In one sense, I grant this with alacrity, and am prepared to go even beyond what Mr. Chesterton postulates. It would need not only a Catholic, but one of rare psychological gifts and casuistic experience, to follow these five columns and summarise their fundamental sense without lapsing into historical nonsense. So far I go; but I respectfully decline to stop half-way, for reasons which I have stated on the first page of a recent book of which he has evidently read the title. If indeed it is forbidden to non-Catholics to attempt to understand and describe the thoughts of Catholics, then (I there argue) this "would land us in the logical absurdity of abandoning Mormon history to the Mormons, Bolshevism to the Bolsheviks, and why not even botany to the plants?"

G G. COULTON.

St. John's College,
   Dec. 4, 1924.

[From *The Cambridge Review*, December 4, 1924.]

MR. G. K. CHESTERTON REPLIES

SIR,—What are we to do with a man who is always reading and has never learnt to read? Well, if Mr.

Coulton really cannot recognise common sense as useful
in history, I will leave the large ground and meet
him on his own ground.   Naturally, I cannot straighten
out all the details he makes crooked; he must continue
laboriously transcribing "moral danger" and "mortal
sin" and calling it irrelevant to be told what his words
mean.   I must keep a straight face while he hovers
round a French bookstall, picking up something by a
real viscount who thought he was supported by a real
bishop in his dislike of waltzing.   Lord Byron's modesty
blushed at waltzing; but I refrain, with iron magna-
nimity, from pressing this point against Protestantism.
Our critic must tell his interminable anecdotes, regularly
missing the point of each, like that excellent point
about popular dances being more dignified than aristocratic ones.   I cannot track a thousand errors in a
thousand words.   But if he demands details, I will take
one detail: the text from St. Thomas Aquinas.   Granted
there are numberless documents I cannot check; but
here is one I can check.   And if he deals with all the
others as he deals with this one, I cheerfully hold myself
free to doubt all his conclusions from beginning to end.

This debate arose as follows.   I said the Puritan was
narrower than the Catholic; I never said a word about
dance-prohibition being "invented in the sixteenth
century."   Mr. Coulton invented the dancing test; and
said he could hardly find the most grudging medieval
toleration of dances.   At the most, he could not find
anything more than that.   In other words, he could
not find St. Thomas Aquinas in his famous medieval
library.   When that little-known writer was discovered
for him, the authority flatly contradicted him.   St.

Thomas does not condemn dancing in any sense whatever. He does not allow it grudgingly. He does not confine it to weddings. He does not do anything that all medievals were described by Mr. Coulton as doing. He *recommends* it as normally necessary and sometimes meritorious, both in the common and the mystical sense; and that *not* only as a mystical exercise, but as done with the common motive of refreshing men for their duty. For the rest, all sane men would say dancing should be done at appropriate times and with appropriate people; most would say a Bishop had better not copy the Bishop of Rumtifoo.

When a man uses so general a phrase as " times of joy, thanksgivings for liberty, weddings and things of that sort," it is obvious that he means "Don't be always dancing, but dance on due occasions." Why say "hujusmodi" at all, if he does not mean that?

Challenged by this fact, my critic gave a wonderful exhibition of "an embarrassed debater's improvisation." He tried desperately to suggest that St. Thomas can hardly have exactly meant what he said. Apparently he must have meant what somebody else said. He must have been "abbreviating" Albertus Magnus, alleged to demand that all such things should be didactic or devotional. But if that was what Albertus said, then most certainly St. Thomas was not repeating what Albertus said. The context conclusively proves it. Whatever else St. Thomas was, he was not quite so inconsequent as Mrs. Nickleby. There was commonly some connection between the end of a sentence and the beginning. And a statement running: "You cannot always be serious; you must have relaxations; see that your utterances are all in praise of God" would amount to saying, "You must sometimes relax; so don't ever relax." Moreover, the critic has entangled himself hopelessly by trying to prove too much. If the whole thing was didactic or devotional, why was it improper for a priest to take part in it?

All his arguments are like that; but I think that sample will be conclusive. I do not know whether Albertus really meant a theological song; not to mention a theological dance. Was a man to stand on one leg in an attitude expressive of Efficient Grace? But suppose I enquire and find he is wrong about Albertus as he is wrong about Aquinas. Then he will tell me the views of Albertus are not to be found in Albertus but in Anselm; those of Anselm not in Anselm, but in Athanasius; and so on, from refuge to refuge, back to some cavern with a Coptic inscription which (were we learned enough to read it) would cure us of our common delusion that men generally put their own opinions into their own books.

That is his method; for the rest, I never dreamed of basing my case on things only Catholics can understand, save as they are things Mr. Coulton cannot explain. One of them is what he calls "winking," and I call a sense of proportion; and nobody will be surprised at his not understanding that. I say the Roman Church is not a sect as the Roman Empire was not a small nationality. I like small nationalities; but it was not. I could correct every sentence thus; but I have preferred to clear up one concrete case. Given time and space, I could dispose of his whole tangle of tail-foremost facts as easily.

Yours, etc.,
G. K. CHESTERTON.

[From *The Cambridge Review*, January 16, 1925.]

The Cambridge Review closed the discussion on January 16th. It was agreed between Mr. Chesterton and Mr. Coulton that they should be allowed one more letter each. These letters are printed below.—A.H.J.

MR. COULTON'S FINAL LETTER

The Guildhall discussion turned on Puritanism; I took the dance as a test case, and have therefore stuck mainly to that. Readers must judge whether it supports Mr. Chesterton's theory that the Church did not preach Puritanism to the people at large before the Reformation. If Mr. Chesterton thinks I am unable to meet the other points he raises, either on the platform or in print, he knows where to find me.

He still relies on inexcusably careless distortions of other men's words. The Viscount says nothing whatever about "*more dignified*" dances; his words are "*less dangerous*," which lend no justification whatever for Mr. Chesterton's "excellent point." St. Thomas Aquinas does not "recommend [the dance] as normally necessary." He recommends sport in general, *ludus*; then, coming to this questionable sport of the dance (*ludus chorealis*), he insists on narrower limitations than some seventeenth century Puritans would have fixed. His direct master in philosophy, Albert, had suggested only four concrete instances of permissible occasions for dance, all four, by their very nature, rare. Aquinas, following his master very closely at every point, mentions two of Albert's permissible occasions, and adds, "and such like." Mr. Chesterton argues that these other *like*

occasions are *not like* the two he has taken from Albert
and the two he has omitted, but must really have been
unlike in one important particular; they must have
been not rare but frequent; and therefore a sentence
which merely *tolerates* dance on two rare occasions
" and such like" may be described as "*recommending it* as
normally necessary." I am grateful to Mr. Chesterton
for his reminder of Mrs. Nickleby.

MR. CHESTERTON'S FINAL REPLY

I may well depart with warm thanks to Mr. Coulton for
confirming my views. It is part of the fun, of course,
that he should split two more of his strange straws. The
Viscount never mentioned dignity: I never said he did.
For the rest, Mr. Coulton argued that even Puritans
might permit dancing on occasions that were religious.
He now says the occasions named were rare. I say St.
Thomas was manifestly not talking of dances that were
religious and not thinking of things that were rare.
He plainly says we should "intersperse" or scatter these
things through our lives, to avoid fatigue. A man could
not avert a nervous breakdown by having been married
twenty years ago. Joanna Southcote could not open her
box for the first time whenever she felt tired. Mr.
Coulton now says that the saint can only mean all the
other sports: but if he meant this strange distinction,
why did he not say so? Why in the world should he
defend a dance which he wished to be rare by an argument
that would encourage it to be frequent?

So with his weird evolutions about the word "like."
Whenever we say "Dance at weddings and such like,"

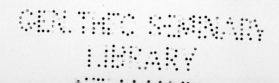

there does remain the abstract ambiguity "Like in what respect?" But the most natural sense would seem to be "Like in being ordinary occasions for dancing." Mr. Coulton passionately asserts that it must mean "At certain long intervals of time." Why?

And now that his whole case hangs by this hair, when even to preserve that, he has to admit an infinity of sports and games, may I respectfully enquire what has become of the old big question which was the only thing I ever discussed in my lecture?

G. K. CHESTERTON.

PRINTED BY W. HEFFER & SONS LTD., CAMBRIDGE, ENGLAND.